THE CHANGING FACE OF WHAT IS NORMAL

expl**O**ratorium®
San Francisco

THE CHANGING

FACE OF

WHAT IS NORMAL

An Exhibition Exploring
Concepts of Normality and Difference

Published by the Exploratorium
Pier 15
San Francisco, CA 94111
exploratorium.edu

Library of Congress Cataloging-in-Publication Data
available upon request.

ISBN 978-0-943451-61-9

Printed in Canada

This book accompanies the Exploratorium exhibition
The *Changing Face of What Is Normal*, April 17, 2013–
April 13, 2014.

CONTENTS

This exhibition is the result of a personal journey. The idea was born during a family trip to St Joseph, Missouri, which included a visit to the Glore Psychiatric Museum, an unusual institution exhibiting psychiatric treatment methods and artifacts. Created by George Glore, who worked at the Missouri Department of Mental Health, the museum features mannequins imprisoned in cages, immersed in baths, and splashed by cellophane sheets standing in for cold blasts of water. But one exhibit in particular sparked my imagination: the Utica Crib. This horizontal cage looked like a child's crib with bars over the top, and it imprisoned a rather gray-faced female mannequin. I work at an interactive museum called the Exploratorium, and I wondered what would it feel like to be stuck in that cage. I tried to imagine how it would be to be restrained inside, not able to bring up my knees or turn over. How would it feel to be forced to lie in one position for days? For weeks or years?

So I asked Pete Scheidl, one of our exhibit technicians, to make one, and it ended up on the Exploratorium floor. Visitors can lie down in it or put someone else in it. (Most often, I find a kid sitting on the top while a sibling lies inside yelling for mom.) As an exhibit, it is not entirely successful, because it's impossible to replicate the feeling of imprisonment of uncertain length in such cramped quarters. But I wanted to see if visitors could make an imaginative leap and think for a moment about what it might have felt like for those who actually experienced it. Is it possible to create an experience that encourages us to walk in someone else's shoes?

That idea led to a further question: Who were the people the mannequins represented? What had they done? Where did they come from? Weren't they, perhaps, just as normal as I was? And *normal* was the word that stuck in my mind. It's a word charged with power. Everyone has an opinion about it; our society is obsessed with wanting to know what is normal. There is the Pulitzer Prize-winning musical *Next to Normal*, a cell phone application called *What Is Normal?*, and at least 30 songs available on iTunes® called *Normal*. People feel a need to know how they measure up to the concept of normality. From

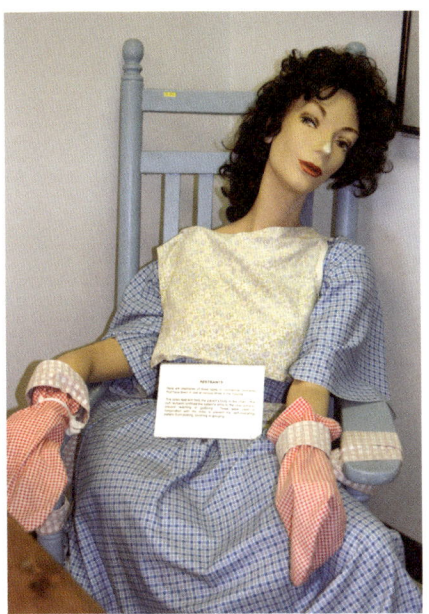

Glore Psychiatric Museum mannequins (2012)

social behavior and health issues to lifestyles and habits, Americans crave to know if we are normal or not, and we respond by either being glad we are *not* normal or relieved that we are.

If you do a web search for *normal,* it's not long before you come across references to the *Diagnostic and Statistical Manual of Mental Disorders,* a book used by psychiatrists, therapists, and clinicians to describe and categorize mental abnormalities. (In fact, if you want to lose an evening in a surprisingly dense topic, search for "DSM controversy"; you'll plunge down a rabbit hole of opinions and discourse.) For a thousand reasons, ranging from legal implications and identity issues to stigmas and insurance claims, this book matters a great deal to a great many people. From professionals to "consumers," people

care about what is included and what is not. I became increasingly convinced that there was an exhibition here somewhere, but I still needed to get to the heart of the matter.

The heart was found in an amazing story of 427 suitcases discovered in 1995, in an attic of the Willard Psychiatric Center in upstate New York. The hospital was being closed, and amidst the scramble, people were trying to decide what was important and preserve what they could. Someone pushed through a door and found a room filled with the suitcases of former patients, covered with pigeon guano, dusty with years. Craig Williams, a historian from the New York State Museum, was called. His directors told him to take 10 for the museum, but he took them all. When I learned of the suitcases, I visited Craig and saw the objects they contained—

shoes, purses, combs and brushes, letters, photographs. They could have been mine. The patients, their owners, could have been me.

Craig told me about Jon Crispin and Karen L. Miller, artists creating work based on the suitcases. Jon was working on a photography collection and had been producing evocative images of the suitcases and their contents. Karen, a psychiatrist and poet, had been interviewing caregivers who had lived and worked at Willard. Many had worked for 30 years in the industry and had seen major changes in the continuum of care. It seemed important to include their voices as well.

The exhibition was taking shape. At this point, it felt like it had three core aspects: an experimental interactive area where visitors could explore the concept of restraint; a "food for thought" area with an overview of the DSM; and an area of the heart, designed to ask people to, as Scout says in *To Kill a Mockingbird,* "climb into [someone else's] skin and walk around in it."

This exhibition and publication are not designed to be comprehensive. They do not attempt to explore the entire landscape or history of the mental health industry, critique a particular view of mental health or illness, or criticize any specific therapeutic approach. Instead, this exhibition is the result of a singular meandering exploration: me, following my nose, getting caught up in stories, meeting amazing people along the way. I hope that you can see yourself, or someone you know, within it. I also hope it encourages dialogue and questions. How does it feel to be labeled? To have words attached to a condition you never understood? Where do you fit on the evolving continuum of normality? What if you found yourself in a place where you couldn't explain your behavior to others, or understand their responses to your actions? What if you were simply caught in the wrong place—a place where the rules of normality are different—around people who don't accept your behavior? As you visit this exhibition or page through this book, I ask that you enter this place of imaginative empathy, a place where you can see a part of yourself.

This project is the product of many people who care deeply about mental health. They come from a range of backgrounds and each has contributed unique ideas and viewpoints. First, thanks to all of the people of Willard: the caregivers and patients and people of Ovid, New York. Thanks to Craig Williams. Thank you, Jon Crispin, for your lovely and sensitive photographs. I want to give special thanks to psychiatrist and poet Karen L. Miller, who wore multiple hats for this project. She knew to include the essential voices of the caregivers and had the brilliant idea of comparing diagnoses then and now. Thanks also to Darby Penney and Peter Stastny, authors of *The Lives They Left Behind: Suitcases from a State Hospital* (2009) for beginning the conversation. Thanks to our DSM contributors, whose opinions about the DSM mirror many of our own.

Thanks also to the West Gallery team, who have been extraordinarily supportive. Thanks particularly to Stephanie Stewart-Bailey, whose contributions cannot be counted on two hands. And thanks to PEERS, an Oakland-based consumer-run organization that inspires hope and contributes to the resiliency and well-being of mental health consumers. They helped us connect with people whose lives are directly and personally touched by these issues; as they like to say, "Nothing about us without us." And lastly, a very special thank you to the Exploratorium for giving me this incredible opportunity, as well as all of the many funders who have supported us through this move to a new home and enabled us to produce our exhibits, programs, and books.

PAMELA WINFREY is a playwright, a Senior Artist at the Exploratorium in San Francisco, as well as Curator of the West Gallery and the exhibition *The Changing Face of What is Normal.*

Normal is a word with a particularly elastic, slippery definition. It's a concept laden with nuance and heavy with significance. *Normal* can signify safety or adherence to the status quo; it can be a reassuring diagnosis or a confirmation that you belong with the rest of us. It can also mean boring, average, unremarkable, run-of-the-mill. As intensely social creatures, we're often powerfully aware of the degree to which we fit within our social contexts. Are we blending in or standing out—and which are we hoping to do? Who among us has not worried whether we're normal (especially in adolescence), and yet also striven, at least occasionally, to stand apart from the crowd?

Some of the word's power comes from what we take as its opposite. *Normal* has vastly different connotations in comparison with words such as *different, exceptional, unusual,* or *abnormal. Different* can be subtle praise or euphemistic put-down; indeed, we may be just as likely to celebrate those who fail to hide their differences ("Think different") as we are to scold them ("Don't rock the boat"). Being labeled *exceptional* can be a powerful compliment. And being

called *unusual* may suggest that you possess a quality—perhaps positive, perhaps negative—that others lack. On the other hand, *abnormal* carries more than a whiff of negative judgment, as if what's "normal" is good and what isn't is correspondingly bad. So when considering what it means to be normal, we often find ourselves asking "compared to what?"

Given the slipperiness of the idea of normality, is there any objective way to define it? Perhaps the simplest assessment of normality might rely on mere frequency: is this look, behavior, or belief common? If so, to some extent, there's a sense in which it's normal. Behaviors that deviate from commonality stand out—and if the culture in which they occur disapproves of them, they can be actively, even violently, discouraged.

But this statistical approach fails to capture much of what makes the concept interesting. For example, behaviors that deviate from some statistical norm are not necessarily frowned upon, and may vary widely with time and context. For example, as this is written, the United States is actively debating the normality of same-sex relationships, and that national conversation has evolved more rapidly than many expected. Moreover, positions on such issues vary widely with geography, ethnicity, and political and religious affiliation.

In other words, *normal* is not universal; it's temporally and culturally variable. We're used to defining normality within familiar surroundings, but stepping out of those contexts reveals how elusive the concept really is. (That's one reason why travel can be so eye-opening: even a simple action or gesture that is completely unremarkable in one context can elicit very strong reactions in another.) And an awareness of cultural and temporal distinctions in assessments of normality shines a light on the critical question of whose definition(s) we're using.

These statistical and cultural approaches to normality center on the apparent fit between the individual and the group. A functional approach would focus instead on *what works*. Does a given action or belief lead to emotional or physical distress? Does it make it difficult for the actor to fit and function within their culture? Questions like these are at the heart of modern medical and psychiatric approaches to helping people cope

with the potentially corrosive results of social or behavioral deviance. And they can also have political ramifications: that an act causes social conflict doesn't necessarily mean that the action should be suppressed or legislated against; if something seems abnormal, perhaps it's the mores and policies of the surrounding society, rather than the individual's actions, that need reassessment.

In addition to different ways of *defining* normality, there have been many different types of explanations *for* abnormality. In centuries past, and in some cultures today (including our own), deviance may be explained as the work of demons or evil spirits. A psychoanalytic view might hold that deviance results largely from powerful but incompletely processed early experiences. And a medical model focuses on biological or genetic roots.

All of these can be useful ways of thinking about normality and deviance, but none completely captures the concept or can draw a line between normality and abnormality that satisfies everyone. The core realization is that normality is not a set of rigidly defined categories but a dynamic range of continua—shaped by cultural forces and powered by our fundamental concern with the relationship between the individual and the social environment. And critically, the first step in any deep exploration of the idea is an analysis of one's own assumptions and reactions. Where do my ideas of normality come from? What are they based on? Which kinds of deviance do I find inspiring, and which make me nervous or repulse me—and why? And if those reactions don't make sense, or cut me off from the world around me, does it make sense to think about them a bit more deeply?

This exhibition, of which this publication is a part, is not intended to provide a single definition of normality, or to resolve the question of whether normality is desirable in any particular context. Instead, we hope it prompts people to think about the concept in new ways, to search for the sources of their own judgments of normality, and to probe their own responses to those who don't seem to fit—including themselves.

HUGH E. MCDONALD is a social psychologist and science writer at the Exploratorium. As Associate Curator of the museum's West Gallery, he oversees the development of exhibits about cognition, emotion, and social behavior.

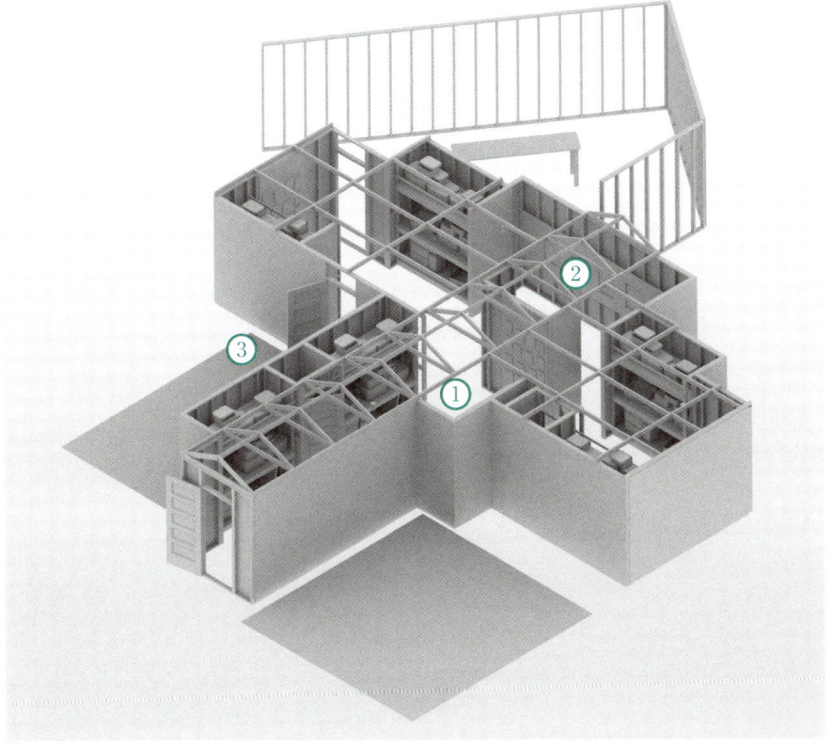

Exhibition Plan for *The Changing Face of What is Normal*
1) The Willard Suitcases
2) The DSM: What Is It, and Why Is It So Controversial?
3) Restraint: Let Me Count The Ways

I

Suitcases, Trunks, and Other Baggage

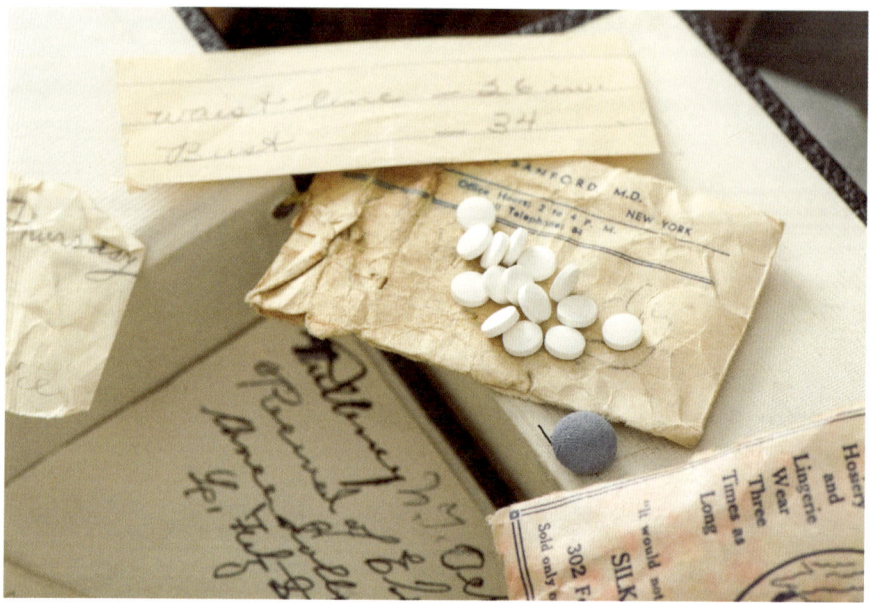

Jon Crispin, *Willard Suitcases* (2012)

Pamela Winfrey

WILLARD: A RESPONSE TO A PROBLEM

"A place like this was called an asylum for a reason. It gave people a rest from whatever environment they had been in. So, like it or not, it had a place in the continuum of treatment."

—CRAIG VON VESSEM, *Willard Psychiatric Center nurse and nurse administrator*

The treatment of people with mental health conditions has always been a complex and challenging issue. Treatments have ranged from hot baths to cold showers and isolation cells to group therapy, and have been impacted by law, public opinion, social activism, and medical and technological innovations such as psychotropic drugs. But the challenges and complexities remain.

Today, the term *asylum* can strike fear in our hearts as a place that restricts freedom, but the original word referred to a place of safety away from the cruelties of life. Accepting the first patients in 1869, Willard Asylum for the Insane* was one of several institutions built in New York in response to the deplorable conditions people were often subjected to in other facilities. (One of the first patients that came to Willard had spent so much time in a chicken coop that he lost the use of his legs.) Officials knew that something had to be done to better care for these people.

Willard, then, was a response to a problem. This rural community tried to improve conditions by providing a safe environment and a meaningful life and work. But over time, a confluence of new psychotropic drugs, new views on humane and effective treatment, new laws designed to protect patients, and the exploding cost of residential care, led to the closure of these large institutions, and "mainstreaming" of many patients. This process of "deinstitutionalization" picked up speed in the 1960s, moving patients to nursing homes, emergency rooms, correctional facilities, the homes of family or friends, or the streets. Some people were able to form groups where they could feel solidarity and kinship and work for political and social change. Others

*The institution's name was changed to Willard State Hospital in 1890 and to Willard Psychiatric Center in 1974.

Courtesy of New York State Museum, New York State Archives, Jon Crispin,
Willard Psychiatric Center (2012)

found themselves without support and with nowhere to go. Willard,
which closed permanently in 1995, was only one of many such institutions to vanish.

Today, if you are suffering from mental challenges, and you are
lucky, you may be housed in a small group home or nursing facility; if
you're very lucky, your family will be able to house and care for you—
although the cost of lifetime residential care has become prohibitive.
Many people who were formerly hidden away enter the public school
system or earn their own living. "Community" is now a larger concept,
with a broader view of what constitutes a normal productive citizen.

But those without a supportive family or funds fare differently.
School guidance counselors, clerics, human resource directors, and
many others struggle to accommodate the growing numbers of people
who suffer without adequate care. Many people find themselves trapped
in the never-ending cycle of a failing system, then thrust out on the
street, and then back into the system again. (Think about that for a
moment: what would you do if you were suddenly without the support
and care your condition requires? If you found yourself alone and on
the street, with no resources? How can anyone who hasn't experienced
this imagine what it must be like?) The problem of the indigent ill that
has existed throughout history continues to plague us today: what
happens to an individual who has no money, no family, and no friends
in a position to help?

One response is to create a network of people who understand
these issues and can navigate the various medical and legal systems

because they have faced similar challenges. Peers Envisioning and Engaging in Recovery Services (PEERS) is just one of the organizations that have formed in response to the need to create a caring community to address this personal and societal crisis. These organizations not only form a close-knit group of colleagues and friends, but they have also created effective political voices that can bring about change in their communities.

WILLARD POSTCARDS

These fading postcards depicting Willard Psychiatric Center were sent by patients to family and friends.

All photographs courtesy of New York State Museum, New York State Archives.

Chapin House-- A Glimpse of South Wing, Willard, N. Y.

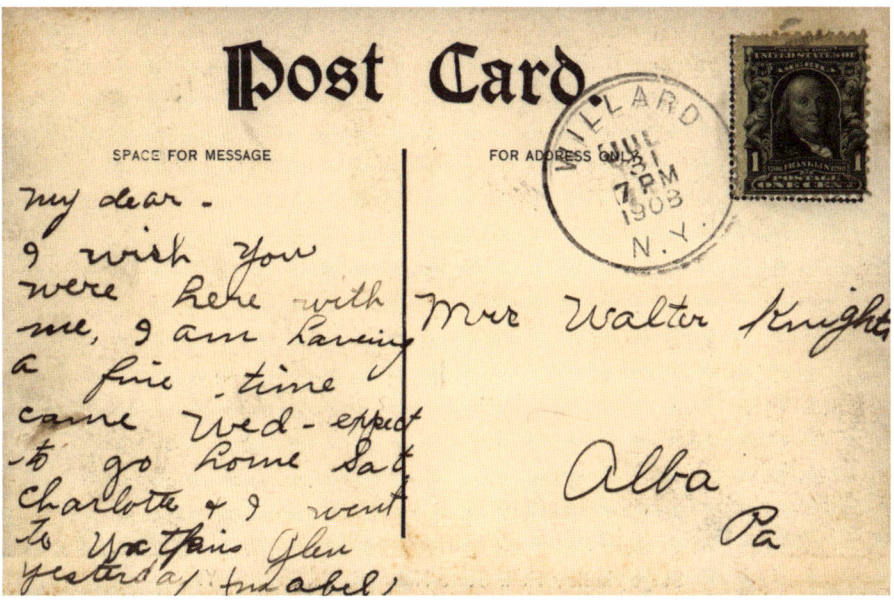

Post Card

SPACE FOR MESSAGE

FOR ADDRESS ONLY

WILLARD
JUL
31
7 PM
1908
N.Y.

my dear -
I wish you
were here with
me, I am haveing
a fine time
came Wed - expect
to go home Sat
Charlotte & I went
to Watkins Glen
yesterday Ina abel

Mrs Walter Knight

Alba
Pa

Fielday sept 1910

Vinelands, State Hospital, Willard, N. Y.

The way they do it at Willard, N. Y. "Roping him in."

Stage Hadley Hall, State Hospital, Willard, N. Y. *Mabel*

Boat Landing Willard, N. Y., Seneca Lake

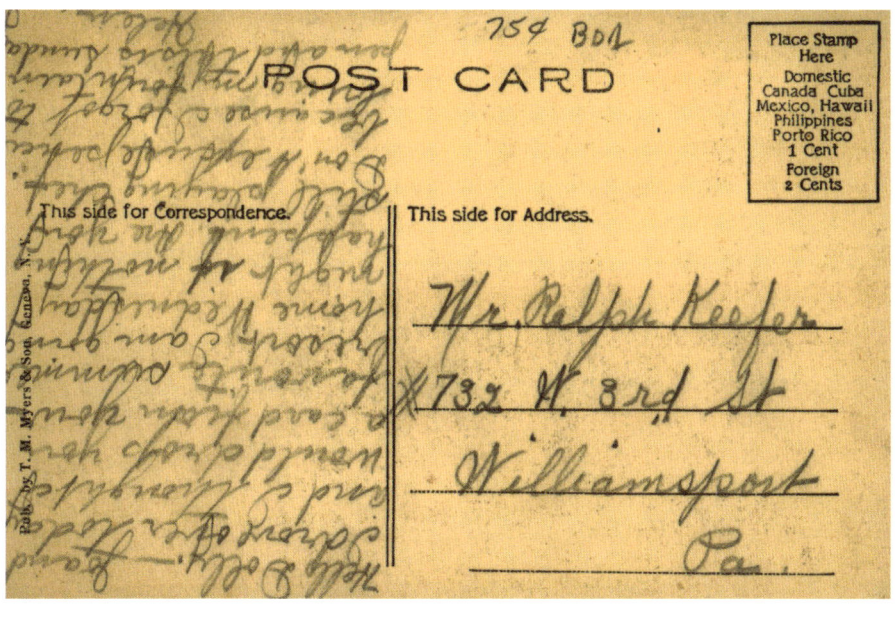

BECAUSE

"How about a poem as to why we need to remember and preserve these people, this stuff?"
—**CRAIG WILLIAMS,** *New York State Museum curator, archivist, and historian*

Because of the wood its smoother edge
because of the grain
because of the groan
of the wood released.
Because of the hair in the brush
the key on a string

*string along strung out
strong dose.*

Because of a seam in silk
because of the lace
of the soft to our touch
if we reach if we touch
on top of the bed a line
of light because of the underneath.

Because of the green brush
the green and shiny comb the swirl
of the green of the box
of hair pins the green mirror
because of the way she wore
her hair we do not know
how she wore her hair
no one wrote it down.

Because it is not a pile it is what
they could not bear
they could not part with

because it is stone cold
because it is hot as a

button button
who's got it?

Because
there is no day like the day
when the leaves
laugh they laughed
when the train
from New York City
wheezed clacked
as it carried them
grown men and women
because grown men were carried
like babies because
they were bedded.

Because there is no bed
like the present
where he where she were
lost they were not
the last
in the slick
of the dark.
You lifted the curtains
pulled them because the
eyes at the window
your mother's eyes,
they were your eyes.

Because when you wake in your bed
and your dream wakes with you
and it follows you like a sick dog.

Because you have waited for mail
because you have waited for news
because you had a new
dress suit hat
that you kept until it
did not fit was no longer
needed had nothing to cover

worth seeing.
Because the sun bleaches the color out
you swallowed bleach
you tore up your throat the road
you went on a tear.

Because of a hand's weight
because we wait.

Because there is never enough
money and money is never the root
of the give of the gone of the

take me out to the—

ten cents a dance—

Because you kept the (railway
theatre laundry traffic wrong)
ticket you kept
coming up with the wrong reason
the wrong mistake.
Because a stranger visited
you because you were a visitor
strange to someone else
you slept in a bed you did not
know and you liked it
you did not.

Sing the how
I lay me down.

Because you went at the wrong
time
because you knew a girl once
and he touched your hair
and someone forgot to give him
a message
she left it behind
and you forgot
and later you missed her.

Because love followed them everywhere.

27

SUITCASES, TRUNKS, AND OTHER BAGGAGE | BECAUSE

KAREN L. MILLER is a psychiatrist and
poet who has researched the patients and
caregivers of Willard in her artistic work.

ARCHIVAL PHOTOGRAPHS

These photographs depict daily life of patients and staff at
Willard. With a farm, machine shop, kitchen, pharmacy, and
theater, the institution was largely self-sufficient.

All photographs courtesy of New York State Museum, New York State Archives, Margaret Ellsworth.

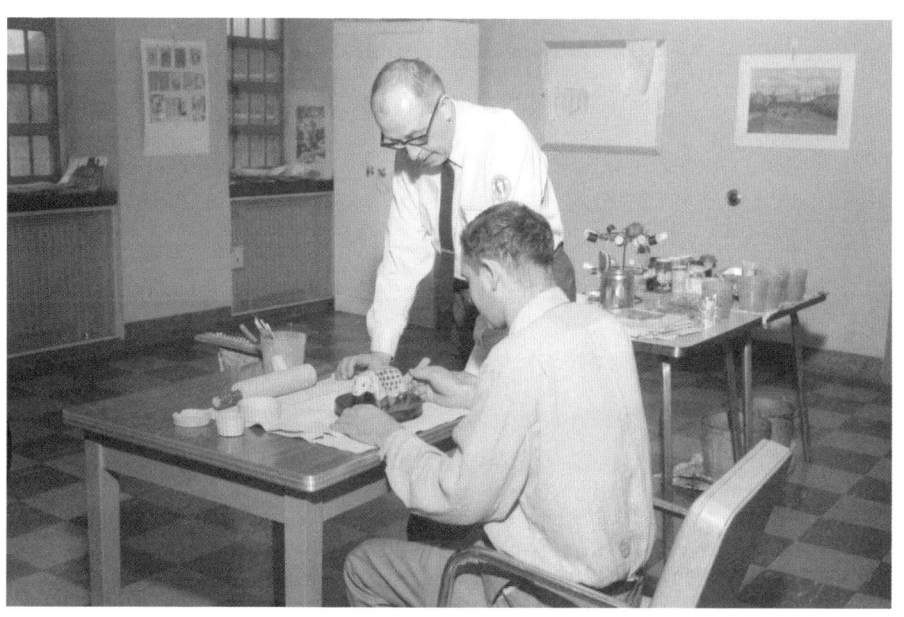

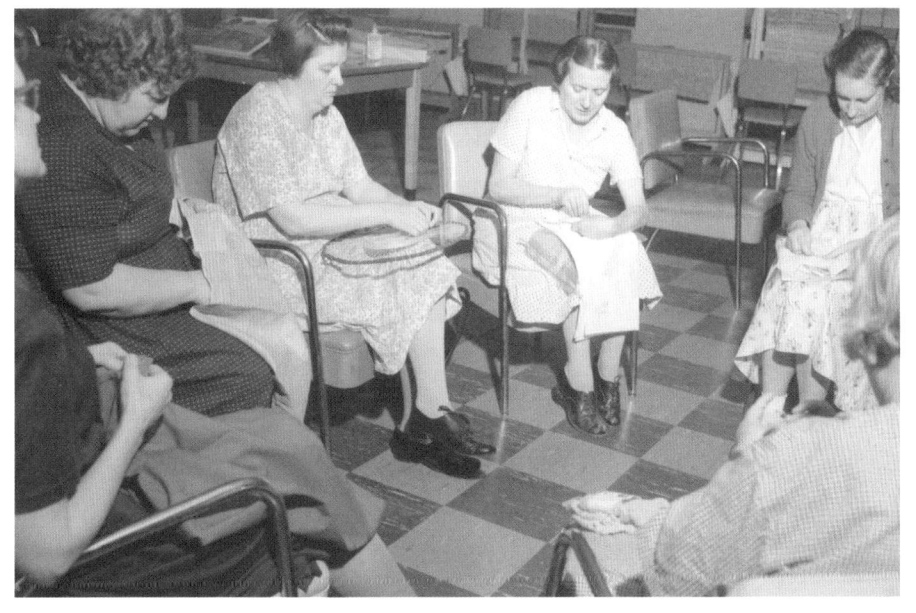

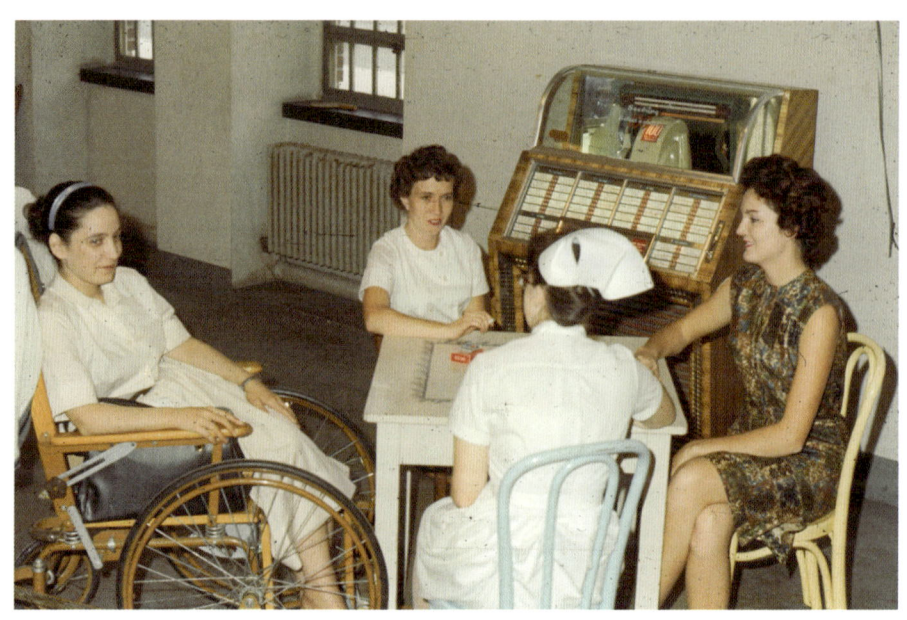

Jon Crispin, *Willard Suitcases* (2012)

FRAGILE HISTORY

Why were they forgotten?

The suitcases sat untouched for decades in an abandoned attic, many just as their owners had left them the day they were admitted to the state hospital. Once behind its walls, society could easily forget about their owners, no longer having to face them on the streets of their communities. And the suitcases' owners *had* been largely forgotten, many while they were living. Many had died there and were buried in unmarked graves in the institutional cemetery. A few Willard security and maintenance staff knew of the suitcases, but their significance was overlooked. The last time the suitcases were administratively recorded was probably in the 1970s, when Chapin Hall, Willard's historic main building, still stood nearby. There must have been other suitcases, and other locations where they were stored (probably in other institutional buildings), though none were ever found.

Today, the Willard suitcases are among the most poignant collections at the New York State Museum. Exhibits, books, plays, sermons, and poems have been based on the collection since they were discovered in 1995. Their contents, and the lives they mirror, speak of individuals— and not just of the original owners. The way we react as individuals to these suitcases says much about societal attitudes toward mental health.

The Willard Asylum of the Insane was founded in 1869 in a bucolic part of upstate New York. The state government had established resources to care for those deemed unable to care for themselves after a diagnosis of mental illness. These individuals were grouped as the "chronic pauper insane," with little expectation of recovery. Left to their own means, many had found themselves chained to the basement walls of county poorhouses before coming to Willard. The state defined its new role to provide, at a minimum, decent ongoing care for as long as needed. For generations, the Willard community put this goal into practice. Willard (then named Willard Psychiatric Center) closed in 1995, after years of *deinstitutionalization*—the transitioning of such patients

Jon Crispin, *Willard Suitcases* (2012)

Jon Crispin, *Willard Suitcases* (2012)

to nonresidential treatment settings—with the hope that its legacy and mission would be carried on by others.

Willard is among my earliest childhood memories. I grew up not far from the facility, within what I would later know as its "catchment" area. When causing trouble, a stern but common warning from parents threatened to "send you to Willard," which, in turn, created a bewildered curiosity about what Willard really was. In the 1950s, a relative of mine was an up-and-coming psychiatrist within the state system, one of a new generation promoting innovative treatments and deinstitutionalization. When he visited during those years, I recall his strident dismay at the troubles of these institutions combined with a just-as-adamant dedication to their improvement. His compassion was inspiring.

In my museum life, I have always been taken with historical themes that cut across time, space, and culture. As photography curator at the New York State Museum, I reach daily for the "big picture," whether in a single image or in an interpretive scheme. The history of our societal relationship to issues of mental health is such a theme, and touches all of us. During the museum's 2004 exhibition on the Willard suitcases, a constant refrain from visitors was that their father/mother/sister/brother had personally confronted such issues. The exhibit encouraged the sharing of these emotions and fostered a deeper understanding of how communities such as Willard had addressed them in the past.

When New York Governor George Pataki announced in February 1995 that Willard Psychiatric Center was to be hastily closed for budget reasons, I contacted Helen (Bunting) Hart, the facility's librarian. As a state agency, one of the mandates of the New York State Museum is to work with other such agencies to document and encourage the public preservation of historically significant collections—and I knew Willard had a wealth of such artifacts. In the 1980s, Helen and I had worked together at the nearby DeWitt Historical Society of Tompkins County, in Ithaca. After she left for Willard, she invited me there on several occasions to give presentations to staff and patients and to tour their old buildings. Helen had become the facility's ad hoc historian, and her library housed a remarkable archive of the institution. Her willingness to help build a lifeboat of institutional heritage for the State Museum led to the suitcases' discovery. Many others soon joined her in her effort to save that heritage.

The staff at Willard was proud of its 125 years of care. Willard had long been the primary employer in a very rural area, and its grounds and buildings were very much part of the regional community. Many staff had grown up alongside the facility, and many had parents and grandparents who had worked there as well. In the spring of 1995, this tradition appeared to be coming to an abrupt end. If, as an employee, you were not being transferred to a more distant state facility, you were to be laid off—and most employees were in the latter category. Nevertheless, the museum found its greatest supporters among the staff; without them, the museum would never have learned of the suitcases or been able to preserve more than a few of them.

At the same time, the museum faced key challenges. The fiscal woes of state government that were forcing Willard's closure were also handicapping the museum. Additionally, the museum had never before dealt with the documentation and preservation of such a collection or theme—and certainly not with such short notice. Somewhat reluctantly, the museum's administrators decided to allow the curatorial team to proceed (with a stern reminder about our limited resources). By early March 1995, museum staffers were regularly making the four-hour drive to Willard from Albany; within a month, several truckloads of artifacts and records had been received, many delivered personally by Willard employees. Willard staffers had also prepared detailed lists of possible additional artifacts and led museum personnel through the buildings in a search for things forgotten.

Coordinating the effort at Willard was Beverly Courtwright, one of the Willard employees who had grown up with the institution. While a child, her family had participated in the Family Care program. Family Care, part of the deinstitutionalization effort, placed patients who were deemed not in need of direct care in nearby private homes. (As Beverly later said, she had eight grandmothers in her home.) Amidst a flurry of activity, Beverly's office was the first place I reported every morning during the Willard closure. A storehouse clerk, she found herself in the logistical center of the closure. With grace and good spirit, she soon assumed responsibility for emptying dozens of buildings and disposing of many truckloads of equipment and supplies. She always made time for the museum's curators. Working closely with her staff, we packed what seemed countless historical artifacts and records. On one of the last mornings of the project, an unusually serious Beverly asked me to join her at the Sheltered Workshop building.

The 19th-century Sheltered Workshop building was also known as the Laboratory, housing several rooms of medical labs on its first floor. The floors above had been used for occupational and recreational therapy. It was among the older extant buildings, the last of a complex that once surrounded Willard's main building, Chapin Hall. That grand 1869 structure had been torn down in the 1980s after a passionate but ultimately unsuccessful preservation struggle. While director of the DeWitt Historical Society, one of my first visits to Willard had included a journey through Chapin before its demolition, sadly realizing little

Jon Crispin, *Willard Suitcases* (2012)

Jon Crispin, *Willard Suitcases* (2012)

Jon Crispin, *Willard Suitcases* (2012)

more could be done at that controversial time. (Indeed, permission to enter the building only came after a call from my psychiatrist uncle to Willard's Director, Dr. Anthony Mustille, a friend and colleague. It was a relationship we resumed in 1995, helping again during a difficult time.)

With flashlight in hand, Beverly led the way to the attic of the Sheltered Workshop building, refusing—or perhaps unable to clearly describe—why we were there. It was a part of the building that clearly had not been used in many years. The large open loft in the attic, starkly empty, was faced at the other end by a brick wall. The wall had one door beyond which Beverly refused to go. (She wouldn't even open the door. Beverly had an exceptional sensitivity to Willard's history and people.) Beyond the door were over 400 suitcases dating from the first decades of the 1900s—covered with dust, flecked with pigeon dung, but filled with the presence of their past owners.

Later, Beverly admitted to not knowing what to do, but knowing what would happen if she told me. Out of respect to their departed owners, she initially felt that perhaps the best course would have been to leave the suitcases undisturbed, letting them be buried in the eventual collapse of the already deteriorating building. My immediate sense was one of awe, and of being privileged to witness these belongings, knowing that they had to be saved quickly. They were largely intact personal time capsules, uniquely capturing the material lives of individuals at a defined moment and place. Many of these people came to Willard bringing all they thought important, not knowing what the next day might bring. When I called my supervisors later that day to tell of the discovery, I was told to sample the collection but take only a very few, perhaps ten. If the others were to be destroyed, so be it. I have always had a difficult time following orders.

Once committed to their preservation, Beverly made sure that the museum would be able to recover all of them, or nearly so. She encouraged other coworkers, many having just been laid off, to go to the attic and help with the rescue. Once again, they cared for the individuals represented by the suitcases. The museum would have never succeeded in this project without that dedication. My most vivid memory is of returning to the attic a few days later, watching several Willard employees efficiently listing and wrapping the suitcases, volunteering to save them. Fragile light came through broken windows and holes in the roof. The heat and dust were oppressive, almost sickening. Staff members were dressed in modern surgical garb (left from the facility's closure) for their own protection. Finally, on April 28, 1995, the transfer documents for the suitcases were signed. (Not all came to the museum; about a dozen suitcases were returned to elderly patients still living at Willard and in the process of being moved to other institutions.)

New though not unexpected issues arose immediately. Some officials at the State Office of Mental Health in Albany were concerned enough about violating patient confidentiality to question the entire transfer. As possible "medical records," the suitcases would have to abide by the same HIPAA-inspired rules that restrict access to all patient information and identity. Perhaps they should be destroyed to protect their owners' privacy? For our collection managers, the suitcases occupied considerable space in an already crowded storage area, and some were dirty and smelly as well. In addition, many were proving to be empty, or nearly so. Why keep those, our managers asked?

Most of all, the contents of the suitcases were already raising provocative questions—and the answers would remain forever sealed in medical files, records which had been transferred at the same time as the suitcases to the museum's sibling agency, the State Archives. If we could never have access to those records, how useful could the contents truly become? In the meantime, many museum volunteers and staff tackled cataloging and conservation issues. In 2008, Sarah Jastremski, Christine Allen, and Kara Chambers, of the museum's curatorial unit, completed the grueling task of cataloging and rehousing all of the suitcases.

The suddenness of Willard's closure, and the completeness of its paper and artifact record, challenged the State Archives and the State Museum to be better prepared. Would other historic state hospitals and asylums have similar stories? In the fall of 1998, a colleague from the State Archives and I met with the executive staff of the Commissioner of the State's Office of Mental Health (OMH). The Commissioner, James Stone, was a former high school history teacher and was himself once a Willard employee. He had a sincere interest in not only preserving that history but in sharing both the good and bad with the public, to learn from the past.

During the meeting, we gave a brief overview of the Willard closure, and I concluded my presentation with images of the suitcases. At that moment, there was an audible gasp from Darby Penney, the head of the Office of Recipient Affairs. Darby is personally and professionally devoted to explaining mental health issues—not through countless case files and reports, but through the stories of people's lives. The Willard suitcases put individual human faces on the complex and abstract debates around mental health, and Darby instantly grasped their significance. With her backing and direction, the OMH sponsored deeper research into the suitcases, releasing the case files to an approved project to better understand the relationship between the suitcase owners and society's attitudes toward mental health. By unlocking those files for museum curators and historians, Darby and OMH psychiatrist Peter

Stastny immeasurably added to our understanding and appreciation of the suitcases. In 2004, the museum opened an exhibition drawing on that research. During its nine-month duration, nearly 900,000 visitors studied the exhibit. Instead of the controversy that some predicted, I found families in the gallery discussing mental health, sometimes even with complete strangers. The museum had become safe territory to confront a very difficult topic.

Has it been correct to share these people's lives? I continue to ask myself that question. Our use of their personal belongings raises privacy concerns that can never be truly answered. Yet the authentic artifact has a special power to create empathy with these individuals. The belongings are so much like ours: letters from parents, family photo albums, best clothes, favorite books. After coming to Willard, the stigma of mental illness isolated so many of them from the rest of society, from us. We forgot them, and we were all worse off as a result. These suit-cases help us remember—and understand.

Beverly Courtwright came to the museum the day of the exhi-bition's opening festivities. That afternoon, she told me that the spirits of the suitcases were well pleased. I believe her.

CRAIG WILLIAMS is Curator of History at the New York State Museum, the home of the Willard Psychiatric Center patient suitcases.

THE CAREGIVERS OF WILLARD

In 2010, psychiatrist and poet Karen L. Miller interviewed many of the caregivers at Willard Psychiatric Center. Many were long-term employees; some had worked there for 30 years or more and had seen major changes in care for people who suffered from mental health issues. All photos courtesy of Jon Crispin (2010).

JANE DOX,
occupational therapist

Willard was a family affair. It was not unusual to find a couple of members from every family up and down this street that worked in the psych center. We got to know each other and I really think they helped support each other like any neighborhood would, but Willard was a lot closer than a lot of them.

WEBB RANKIN,
registered nurse and nursing teacher

If you could see the original admission book for the hospital as I did, it was extremely interesting because they had the name of the person and the occupation, where they came from—all of this listed right across, and so many of them they were from the same county. What was their occupation? Pauper. In other words, you could say that that county just emptied their poorhouse.

EUGENE CARROLL,
therapy aide

CHRIS CARROLL,
director of nursing

Gene could tell you about when he was a child. People would come to work over here and the patients would go over there. Patients would work in the houses, on the street. They would mow lawns, plant gardens. People would come to work. Patients would go to work. They shared their skills. That was a long time ago.

When I came here, it was really the beginning of tranquilizers. The very beginning and we didn't know about dosages. And we didn't know about the side effects. In a way we manufactured some disabilities in that people ended up with tardive dyskinesia.* And we couldn't reverse it and we couldn't change it. And their appearance was changed and everything was changed for them. I always liken that to the birth control pill since they didn't know what dosage to use. They used way too big dosages. There were deaths. With the tranquilizers, we didn't know and we had to learn, and it wasn't Willard that had to learn, it was *everyone* that had to learn how to manage it.

PAUL (JERRY) WESTERVELT,
plant superintendent

The first patient was brought here in chains and was a lady, and the last one to leave was a lady, and I didn't realize she was leaving so early that morning or I'd have gone and gotten her a bouquet, but I didn't have time, so I went out to the rose bed and I got some roses and I gave her a handful. So the first one came in chains and the last one left with roses.

JULIE PRENTICE,
therapy aide and LPN

You saw so many things and you wanted to fix the world and you wanted to make everybody better and you kind of realized you couldn't. So you couldn't give all your heart to everybody, but you could sure make a difference with a lot of people. I think it made you tough because you worked so hard. Physical, physical, physical labor. You always wanted to take good care. You could think about it as everybody had their favorites and you should never have favorites. But everybody had their favorites. So everybody was somebody's favorite. So everybody was covered.

*Dyskinesia is a serious side effect of long-term use of antipsychotic medications characterized by involuntary repetitive movements.

SARAH (SALLY) DAWLEY,
therapy aide

And I know one morning at breakfast—this was in the South Wing, there were all these patients that were—of course that was before they had any kind of medication really—they had shock treatment, but that didn't do too much for them. I remember this one patient at breakfast that morning, started picking up these big heavy cups and throwing them against the wall. And she was throwing cups against the wall and they were breaking. Everybody was so upset. Well, there were two of the nurses there—aides or something—nice big heavy women. They ran over and got this patient and took her out, she was probably put in a straitjacket, or else locked up.

The trouble with tranquilizers, it quieted them down and then it quieted them down too much. They would sit around and drool and be in a coma-like state. That was bad, very bad.

SARAH'S MORNING STORY

Dedicated to the generations of therapy aides at Willard Psychiatric Center.

I leave the house, the children's voices
follow me, then fade as I walk down
the village road, look right to see the lake
beyond the trees. The road rises
into open field, the outskirts of the grounds.
Now I turn to see the whole, the lake's
soft shimmer under dull sky, the red brick towers
of the hospital. Some days I see the deer,
white shadows in the dawn, and farther
off other, human figures. Then the screams.
I know whose scream is whose, whose night
misery will claim me first. For a moment, I am still,
I stand between. The crossing seems—
a breaking— into *them*—their dreams—
no horizons there.

LIFE IN AN AGE OF DEINSTITUTIONALIZATION

When residential care facilities like Willard close, former patients may face uncertain circumstances. Families care for some, but others find themselves homeless or ensnared in the criminal justice system.

Elisabeth Washburn, *AMHI* (1994)
According to this former patient of the Augusta Maine Mental Health Institute, hospital overcrowding led to her homelessness.

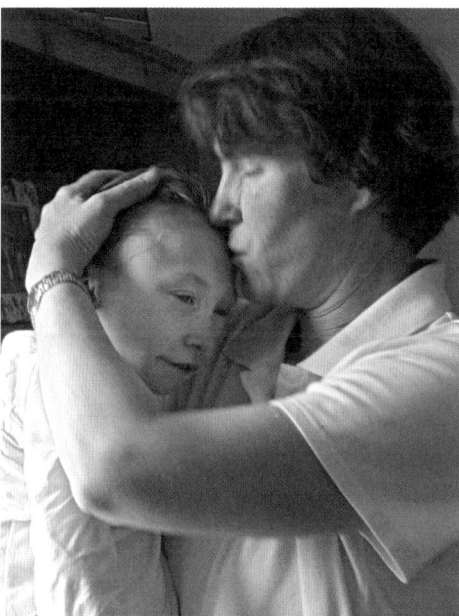

Andrea Mellen, *Molly and Mom* (2008)
Molly is severely disabled and unable to communicate verbally. Rather than institutionalizing her, her family takes care of her at home.

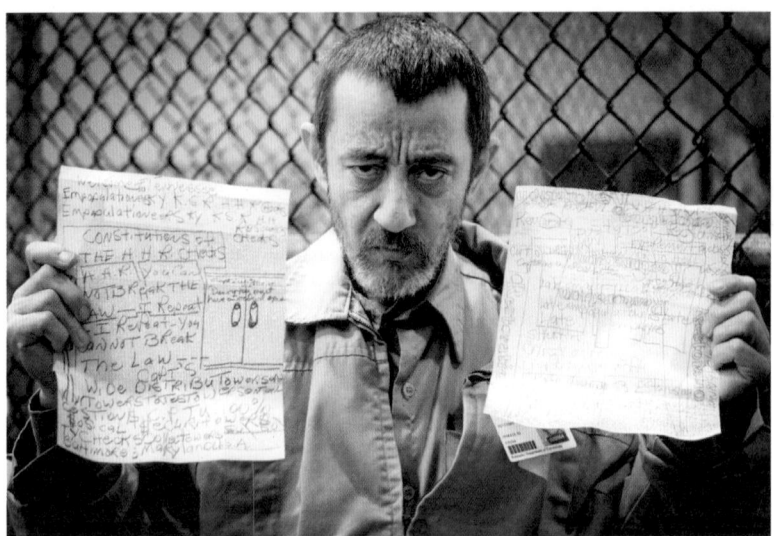

Jenn Ackerman, *Danny*, from *After De-Institutionalization: Images of Homeless or People in a State of Neglect* (2008)

Without adequate care, many U.S. prisons have become defacto holding centers for people with mental health needs, some severe. Danny Castile holds up his own drawings and writing that he claims are invaluable to the Department of Corrections and the judge who sentenced him to life. —photographer Jenn Ackerman

Susan Schwartzenberg, *David Bass and Family*, from *Becoming Citizens: Family Life and the Politics of Disability* (2004)

David was brought up in a regular environment, not in an institutional environment. He participated in all of our family activities. We came together on holidays so he learned a lot of things that he would never have learned in an institution. He listened to our language, he saw the kind of games we played. He was a part of the family, he wasn't isolated, he wasn't kept away. He enjoyed the same experiences, from camping, to boating, to everything. — David's uncle Rosco Bass

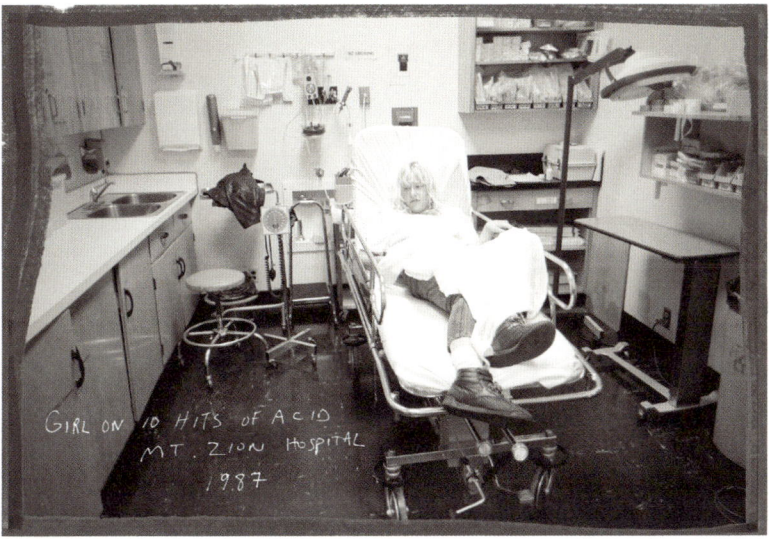

Jim Goldberg, *10 Hits of Acid* (1987)

This homeless woman was discovered on a San Francisco street in a severe psychotic state. She was admitted to the Psychiatric Crisis Clinic at Mount Zion Hospital, which provided emergency care to indigent patients.

II

Defining Normality

Hugh E. McDonald

THE DSM: WHAT IS IT, AND WHY IS IT SO CONTROVERSIAL?

The *Diagnostic and Statistical Manual of Mental Disorders*, popularly known as the DSM, is often problematically referred to as the "bible" of the mental health professions—and as with that older document, its accuracy is hotly questioned and its history of revisions spurs enduring arguments. That controversy flared anew with the Manual's latest revision, the DSM-V, scheduled for publication in 2013.

The DSM, published by the American Psychiatric Association (APA), is an extensive categorization of the characteristics of a wide variety of cognitive, emotional, and behavioral disorders. At its heart is a seemingly straightforward idea: if these disorders are to be effectively treated at both individual and societal levels, the mental health field needs a common tool for assessing psychiatric problems and a common language with which practitioners can discuss them. Clinicians can't work together, or learn from each other, without sharing a basic approach to describing key symptoms and diagnoses. And although the DSM does not specify treatments for the disorders it describes, standardizing descriptions of symptoms makes large-scale research on the effectiveness of different treatments possible.

The Manual has undergone numerous revisions since the first edition was published in 1952. New and revised diagnoses and organizational systems are prompted by research in clinical practice and neuroscience, discussed by clinicians and scientists from a wide range of fields, and approved by the APA Board of Trustees. Its evolution reflects many changes in the way mental health professionals view psychological and behavioral disorders.

But if the DSM is really just a detailed list of symptoms and diagnostic categories, why is it so controversial? Many objections have been raised over the years. Some center on the scientific validity and reliability of the diagnoses it contains. (*Validity* is an index of whether a given assessment tool actually measures what it's intended to measure; *reliability* is an index of whether different clinicians or researchers using the same tool will reach the same conclusions about a given situation.) Others focus on potential conflicts of interest among clinicians, researchers, and others with vested interests (such as the pharmaceutical industry), or on possible cultural biases within the body of researchers who ultimately ratify its conclusions.

Although disagreements about these questions can be highly nuanced, many tend to revolve around a broader philosophical concern: classifying the infinitely complex world of psychological experience and behavioral variability into a limited set of categories may seem a one-size-fits-all approach that ignores human individuality. Boiled down to its basics, the DSM suggests that if a person engages in behavior x for time y, they have a disorder called z. Although we may be comfortable with (or resigned to) a "checklist" methodology when it comes to *physical* maladies, many remain uncomfortable with the idea of applying this approach to thoughts, feelings, and behaviors. The key concern is that when a label sums up the psychological world of an individual, we're in danger of missing the details of the tree for the sameness of the forest. Moreover, there's a real worry that this approach can pathologize behavior that may be essentially normal; for example, someone who's shy "has" a social phobia or anxiety disorder; where once we might have said that "boys will be boys," we now diagnose ADHD.

These concerns are not merely theoretical. DSM-based diagnoses have real consequences for individuals and society. For many, such a diagnosis opens the door to treatment that may alleviate suffering and help them function within their communities. If a person is suffering or behaving destructively, but the DSM does not provide adequate guidance, the client may find treatment inaccessible, with unfortunate or even tragic consequences. On the other hand, over- or misdiagnosis may waste treatment and expose patients to additional risks; some diagnoses may also affect decisions about criminal incarceration or have other legal implications. More broadly, mental health diagnoses, and any social stigma associated with them, become part of a person's permanent medical record, following individuals from place to place more persistently than ever before. These complex balances—concerns over the effects of broad-brushed labeling on the one hand; the need to find more accurate ways to describe and thus treat sufferers on the other—are constantly navigated by clinicians who use and revise documents like the DSM.

It's not the goal of this exhibition to support or condemn the DSM, or to advocate for any specific approach to assessing or treating psychiatric conditions. Instead, our goal is to prompt reflection on the broader questions raised when people attempt to classify and categorize human thought and behavior in any domain. In a way, the questions raised here reflect an enduring concern spanning *all* domains of science: the calculation of the relative importance of false positives and false negatives. The former describe situations in which something absent is mistakenly thought to be present; the latter, situations in which something real is missed or obscured. In this context, the risk of the former centers on the effects of unjustified labeling; the danger of the latter on missing an opportunity to help someone who could possibly be helped. The DSM, and the controversy surrounding it, offers us all an opportunity to reflect on our calculation of these kinds of costs and benefits—for our society and for ourselves.

SIX PERSPECTIVES ON THE DSM

The DSM has been controversial since its first printing in 1952, both because it attempts to standardize descriptions of what are intensely personal experiences and because it plays a fundamental role in the process through which clients obtain treatment. These viewpoints are personal, and, like the DSM itself, illustrate the complexity of trying to define and name the nuances of the human condition.

DAVID ALLYN YOUNG

David Young is the Executive Director for the San Francisco Region at Edgewood Center for Children and Families. Dr. Young is a practicing clinical health psychologist, assistant professor, and social entrepreneur in the effort to leverage social media and web based/mobile technologies for human service applications.

The DSM is merely a concise and reliable way to categorize a set of symptoms and behaviors in order to determine the best course of treatment. A psychiatric diagnosis is only applicable when a person's thoughts, feelings, and behavior are so severe that [they are] interfering with their ability to take care of themselves or function at work, school, or in social relationships. The DSM gives professionals a scientifically supported decision tool in choosing the best interventions that have worked successfully for most people with that specific condition. But ultimately, it's important to remember that in treatment you are working with individuals with their own feelings and beliefs about what they are experiencing and within a cultural and social context. The "art" in being a psychotherapist is knowing when to rigorously adhere to the evidence-based treatment, and when to vary your interventions in order to successfully meet the needs of that individual client.

Mental health professionals have expert knowledge and training in the field. But we are also regular people with our own personal struggles and human flaws. Psychological healing does not happen through a mechanical application of techniques on a passive recipient. It requires the "nonspecific" factors of empathy, mutual respect, and compassion.

The most important thing for me to communicate as a professional who has dedicated most of my life, heart, and soul into this field, is it's helpful for people to know that mental disorders are something that are part of the human experience. There is no moral judgment on struggling with life. Research shows that at any point in time, about a third of the population would have a diagnosable disorder. And so what is actualy normal or not is just whether or not someone is struggling or in pain at the time of making a diagnosis.

ANDREA CRAVER

Andrea Craver went into therapy for social anxiety disorder in 2009. Being diagnosed and treated improved her outlook on life. She was so moved by her own transformation that she is studying to become a therapist herself.

I remember it actually made me feel *more* normal to be diagnosed as something. Like, oh okay, there is actually a disorder out there that explains my experiences. It made me feel like I am not just weird and it was good to know that there are many people going through the same things I am going through. For me, being diagnosed was kind of a positive thing.

I think that using the DSM can be a double-sided coin. On the one hand, it could make it a lot easier for therapists to find treatment for a person. On the other hand, each person is a different individual and might respond very differently to whatever treatments are there. It is the responsibility of the therapist to get to know the patient enough to say, "Well, this medicine isn't going to work for this person so we need to try a different approach." As for another person with the same disorder, therapy might not work for them where chemicals would. So as long as the DSM is a tool that is used properly, it is a good thing.

KAREN L. MILLER

Karen L. Miller is a child and adult psychiatrist who worked for thirty years in hospitals and clinics in Massachusetts. She is now in private practice as a therapist and physician. She is also a poet.

Critics complain that the DSM invites inappropriate diagnosis and an overreliance on medication. While the unwarranted use of psychoactive medication does exist, the DSM is not entirely to blame. As a psychiatrist working in clinics in impoverished communities, I have witnessed the lives of afflicted children and adults who had limited access to the services and care that they required. In such a situation, medication becomes the only resource available that makes it possible for them to function in school, at work, and at home. Current policy has substituted medication for the asylums. The relentless direct advertising of prescription psychoactive medication has made drugs seem like the only reliable solution.

The DSM is a tool, and it can be a useful tool. But it is only one of many resources available to a clinician. While potentially reductive, a diagnosis can give coherence to someone's symptoms and can suggest approaches to treatment. A diagnosis cannot, however, fully describe an individual's experience or appreciate one's complexity as a human being.

SALLY ZINMANN

Sally Zinmann has been an activist in the mental health consumer movement for over 35 years. She traces her activism to her own experience in the mental health system, and being labeled a paranoid schizophrenic. In the 1970s, she was restrained in a basement against her will, beaten, and abused. Her resolve to change the conditions for those with mental health challenges was formed by this experience.

The DSM has now diagnosed so many human behaviors that no single person in this world could not be labeled with a diagnosis at some point in their lives; it's just that they have not been to a psychiatrist.

The DSM leads to pathologizing human behavior, to stigma and discrimination, to biological treatment instead of dealing with whole human beings, with the trauma in their lives and all of their needs and desires. It justifies forced treatment and coercion by other people. It tells you there is a scientific base to your very human behavior. These are all kinds of unintended, or maybe intended, consequences of using it.

The DSM tries to establish a scientific basis for social norms. A really good example, which I think many people know, was that homosexuality was once deemed a mental illness. This was voted out of the DSM sometime in the early '70s or the late '80s, and from then on, any kind of reference to homosexuality was determined not to be a mental illness. This example is totally based on our social and cultural norms. These are not scientific definitions. They are definitions of what people consider to be normal. [Ed.: The diagnosis of homosexuality was eliminated from the DSM in 1973.]

JADER TADEFA

Jader Tadefa is the Tobacco Harm Reduction Coordinator for Peers Envisioning and Engaging in Recovery Services (PEERS). Jader was diagnosed with schizoaffective disorder and has been in the mental health community for 20 years. He works to inspire people by telling stories of his personal struggles with homelessness and substance abuse. He suggests that sometimes people bury their disorders with alcohol or drug use and that this can lead to misdiagnosis of the deeper disorder.

The treatment of people with mental health issues is usually unfair and biased. We are human beings just like anyone else. We are not a diagnosis.

I've noticed that some people with bipolar disorder sometimes might say, "Oh, at least I'm not schizophrenic. At least I'm not talking to myself and, you know, doing, quote-unquote erratic things and such," when actually, I believe that we all could have mental health issues at some point in their life. As far as the DSM-IV and V, if they serve to help people, that's fine, and that's great. But if they serve to categorize us and label us, and that's all we're seen as, then I believe that is not a good use for that book, or a good use of the terminology for any type of diagnosis. If the DSM doesn't serve to help somebody and to help them move forward in their life, you know, build them, if it's only making them want to be categorized—not want to be, but, if it makes them have to associate with some sort of category or label in order to function, I don't think that that's very healthy.

I used to not really mind people calling me derogatory names because of my mental health issue. And I might have told myself I didn't mind, but now when I think about it, I really believe that through working with PEERS and fighting stigma and discrimination toward the mental health community, I find it really unnecessary to refer to people with mental health issues, be it schizophrenia or bipolar or post-traumatic stress disorder, or any other mental health issue, as crazy or insane—I feel it very unnecessary to refer to us that way.

TANYA LURHMANN

Tanya Luhrmann is a psychological anthropologist best known for her studies of modern-day witches, charismatic Christians, and psychiatrists. Much of her work focuses on the way that ideas held in the mind come to seem externally real to people, and the way that ideas about the mind affect mental experience.

There is a lot of social stuff involved in diagnosis. There's a lot of real knowledge about the body and the brain and the mind and the way that we're different from each other. But there's also a lot of social expectation about what *normal* is, how *normal* defines what a psychiatric diagnosis is, and how the labels themselves carry social meaning.

Categories are really useful. It's how human beings think. As we make our way through the world, we organize our world. We see people in groups. We prototype. And we are forced, almost by the very way we think, to define people as normal or not normal. That's helpful. It helps us predict what's going to happen. This helps us function in the world. But labels are costly, particularly if they're labels that pick out something that is full of pain, suffering, or difficulty. Labels help us identify people who are in pain, but they can lead us to fear people. They can lead us to think that those people are not truly human. They can lead us to make things worse for the very people we want to reach out and help.

As there aren't physical markers that can distinguish psychiatric illness from so-called normal life, the DSM is a manual that lays out criteria through which we can identify people who are not normal. The DSM was designed by a smart, capable, sophisticated committee, and now committees after committees after committees. People drew together clinicians who had spent a lot of time treating people with psychiatric illness, to define, "What should depression be? What should schizophrenia be? What should bipolar disorder be?" But most people live in the gray between the categories. The DSM helps us see more clearly, but one of the things that it helps us do is to make people more like each other than they necessarily are, and make us interpret them as more like a diagnostic category than they really should be.

BEYOND THE BRAIN

By the time I met her, Susan was a success story. She was a student at the local community college. She had her own apartment, and she kept it in reasonable shape. She did not drink, at least not much, and she did not use drugs, if you did not count marijuana. She was a big, imposing, black woman who defended herself aggressively on the street, but she had not been jailed for years. All this was striking because Susan clearly met criteria for a diagnosis of schizophrenia, the most severe and debilitating of our psychiatric disorders. She thought that people listened to her through the heating pipes in her apartment. She heard them muttering mean remarks. Sometimes she thought she was part of a government experiment that was beaming rays on black people, a kind of technological Tuskegee. She felt those rays pressing down so hard on her head that it hurt. Yet she had not been hospitalized since she got her own apartment, even though she took no medication and saw no psychiatrists. That apartment was the most effective antipsychotic she had ever taken.

Twenty years ago, most psychiatrists would have agreed that Susan had a brain disorder for which the only reasonable treatment was medication. They had learned to reject the old psychoanalytic ideas about schizophrenia, and for good reasons. When psychoanalysis dominated American psychiatry in the mid-20th century, psychiatrists believed that this terrible illness, with its characteristic combination of hallucinations (usually auditory), delusions, and deterioration in work and social life, arose out of the patient's own emotional conflict. Such patients were unable to reconcile their intense longing for intimacy with their fear of closeness. The science mostly blamed the mother. She was "schizophrenogenic." She delivered conflicting messages of hope and rejection and her own ambivalence drove her child, unable to know what was real, into the paralyzed world of madness. It became standard practice in American psychiatry to regard the mother as the cause of the child's psychosis, and standard practice to treat schizophrenia with psychoanalysis to counteract her grim influence. The standard practice often failed.

The 1980s saw a revolution in psychiatric science, and it brought an enormous excitement about what the new biomedical approach to serious psychiatric illness could offer to patients like Susan. The National Institute of Mental Health called the 1990s the "decade of the brain" as a way of signaling how much psychiatry had changed since its tweedy psychoanalytic days. Psychoanalysis and even psychotherapy were said to be on their way out. Psychiatry would focus on real disease, and its research would pinpoint the biochemical causes of illness and neatly design drugs to target them.

Schizophrenia became a poster child for the new approach, for it was the illness that the previous psychoanalytic era had most spectacularly failed to cure. Psychiatrists came to see how blame was assigned to the schizophrenogenic mother as an unforgivable sin. Such mothers, they realized, had not only been forced to struggle with losing a child to madness, but with the self-denigration and doubt that came from being told that they had caused the misery in the first place. The pain of this mistake still reverberates throughout the profession. Many psychiatrists still think of themselves as fighting the battle against the idea of the schizophrenogenic mother. In psychiatry it became not only incorrect but morally wrong to see the parents as responsible for their child's illness. I remember talking to a young psychiatrist in the late 1990s, back when I was doing an anthropological study on psychiatric training. I asked him what he would want non-psychiatrists to know about psychiatry. "Tell them," he said to me, "that schizophrenia is no one's fault."

It is now clear that the simple biomedical approach to serious psychiatric illness has failed in turn. At least, the bold dream that these illnesses would be understood as brain disorders with clearly identifiable genetic causes and clear, targeted pharmacological interventions—what some researchers call the bio-bio-bio model: brain lesion, genetic cause, pharmacological cure—has faded into mist. To be sure, it would be too strong to say that we should no longer think of schizophrenia as a brain disease. One often has a profound sense, when confronted with a person diagnosed with schizophrenia, that something has gone badly wrong with the brain.

Yet the outcome of two decades of serious psychiatric science is that schizophrenia now appears to be a complex outcome of many unrelated causes—the genes you inherit, but also whether your mom fell ill during her pregnancy, whether you got beaten up as a child or were stressed as an adolescent, even how much sun your skin has seen. It's not just about the brain. It's not just about genes. In fact, schizophrenia looks more and more like diabetes. A messy array of risk factors predisposes someone to develop diabetes: smoking, being overweight, collecting fat around the middle rather than on the hips, high blood pressure, and yes, family history. These risk factors are not intrinsically connected to one another. Some of them have something to do with genes, but most of them do not. In fact they hang together so loosely that physicians now speak of a metabolic "syndrome," something far looser and vaguer than an "illness," let alone a "disease." Psychiatric researchers increasingly think about schizophrenia in similar terms.

And so the schizophrenogenic mother is back. Not in the flesh, perhaps. Few clinicians talk anymore about cold, rejecting mothers—"refrigerator" mothers, to use the old psychoanalytic tag. But they talk about stress and trauma and culture. They talk about childhood adversity—being beaten, bullied or sexually abused, the kind of thing that the idea of the schizophrenogenic mother was meant to capture, although in the new research the assault is physical and the abuser is likely male. They recognize that having a decent/secure place to live is sometimes more important than medication. Increasingly, the important research is done not only in the laboratory, but also in the field, by epidemiologists and even anthropologists. What happened?

The first reason the tide turned is that the newer, targeted medications did not work very well. It is true that about a third of those who take antipsychotics improve markedly. But antipsychotics are not very pleasant to take. They can make your skin crawl as if ants were scuttling underneath the surface. They can make you feel dull and bloated. And while they damp down the horrifying hallucinations that can make someone's life a misery—harsh voices whispering "you're stupid" dozens of times throughout the day, so audible that the sufferer turns to see who spoke—it is not as if the drugs restore most people to the way they were before they fell sick. Most people on antipsychotic medication are so sluggish that they are lucky if they can work at menial jobs. Even when the drugs are effective, they don't remove all the symptoms of the illness—and that turns out to be nearly as true for the new generation wonder drugs as it was for the older ones.

The second reason that the tide turned against the simple biomedical model is that the search for a genetic explanation fell apart. Genes are clearly involved in schizophrenia. The child of someone with schizophrenia has a tenfold increase in the risk of developing the disorder; the identical twin of someone with schizophrenia has a one in two chance of falling ill. But the increased risk that a child of someone with Huntington's chorea—a terrible convulsive disorder caused by a single inherited gene—will go on to develop the disease goes up by a factor of

10,000. If you inherit the gene, you will die of the disease. Schizophrenia isn't like that. In fact the effort to narrow the number of genes that may play a role has been frustratingly daunting. A leading researcher on the genetics of schizophrenia, Ridha Joober, has argued that there are so many genes involved and the effects of any one gene are so small that the serious scientist working in the field should devote his or her time solely to identifying genes that can be shown not to be relevant. Indeed, the number of implicated genes is so great that Schizophrenia Forum, an excellent website devoted to organizing the scientific research on schizophrenia—useful, as there have been 50,000 articles on schizophrenia published in the last two decades—has what Joober called a "gene of the week" section. Another scientist, Robin Murray, one of the most prominent schizophrenia researchers in Europe, pointed out that this meant that you could track the scientific status of a gene the way you track the performance of a football team. He said that he liked to go online to the Schizophrenia Forum to see how his favorite genes were faring.

The third reason is that a small cadre of psychiatric epidemiologists and anthropologists has made clear that culture really matters. Schizophrenia has a more benign course and outcome in the developing world. The best data come from India. In the study that established the difference, when researchers looked at people two years after they first showed up at the hospital for care, they were significantly better on most outcome measures than their comparable group in the West. They had fewer symptoms, took less medication, and were more likely to be employed and married. The results were dissected, reanalyzed, and then replicated—not in a tranquil Hindu village, but in the chaotic urban tangle of modern Chennai. No one really knows why, but increasingly, psychiatric scientists are willing to attribute the better outcomes to social factors. For one thing, families are far more involved in the ill person's care in India. They come to all the appointments, manage the medications, and allow the patients to live with them indefinitely. Compared to Europeans and Americans, they yell at the patients less. And they often don't use the label of "schizophrenia" to describe their ill family members, even if that's the diagnosis the doctors use.

Meanwhile, the most remarkable recent epidemiological finding is that some migrants fall ill with schizophrenia more often than the countrymen they leave behind or those to whose lands they come. Dark-skinned migrants to Europe, mostly from the Caribbean or sub-Saharan Africa, have a risk for schizophrenia that is as much as 10 times higher than that of white Europeans. Some observers think that the epidemiological finding is a stark story about the way racism gets under the skin and drives people mad. But it is probably more complicated than that. A young anthropologist, Johanne Eliacin, spent two years doing anthropological fieldwork in the London community of African Caribbean migrants. She certainly saw racism, and she felt viscerally her subjects' stinging sense of being unwanted and out of place. But she also saw a social world shot through with hostility and anger, in which people were isolated and often intensely lonely.

All this—the disenchantment with the new generation antipsychotics, the failure to find a clear genetic cause, the discovery of social causation in schizophrenia, the increasing dismay at the comparatively poor outcomes from schizophrenia in our own health care system—has produced a backlash against the simple biomedical approach to diagnosing and treating schizophrenia. Increasingly, treatment for schizophrenia presumes that something social is involved in its cause and ought to be involved in its cure.

You can see this backlash most clearly in the Recovery movement, which explicitly embraces the idea that the very way you imagine an illness will affect the way you experience it—an idea that seems, well, almost psychoanalytic. The movement officially arrived in 2003, when the Bush administration issued a federal mandate promoting "recovery-oriented services." Treatment providers paid by Medicare and Medicaid were told that schizophrenia would no longer be understood as an illness with a chronic and debilitating course, a death sentence for the mind. Instead, patients and mental health professionals were instructed to believe that people with schizophrenia could live as effective members of a community, able to work and to be valued. They were to replace the expectation of permanent impairment with hope. As the movement's manifesto defined it, "recovery is a process, a way of life, an attitude, and a way of approaching the day's challenges." The recovery movement has been the most influential patient-driven movement in decades.

In practice, this has meant that many programs and day treatment centers once run by non-patient staff have been turned over to clients (so as to empower them), and that staff allow clients to make more decisions about how to spend their money and what to do with their time. This has not been without bumps. Clients have not always made good choices; staff have been reluctant to allow them a free hand.

But the point is that the very idea of the recovery intervention upends the bio-bio-bio vision. Clients are certainly encouraged to take their medication, but the real therapeutic change is thought to come through something social: something people learn to do, say, and believe.

That is also true for other innovative strategies to treat schizophrenia. In Europe, the Hearing Voices network teaches people who hear distressing voices to negotiate with them. They are taught to treat the voices as if they were people: to talk with them, and make deals with them, as if the voices had the ability to act and decide on their own. This runs completely counter to the simple biomedical model of psychiatric illness, which presumes that voices are meaningless symptoms, ephemeral sequelae of lesions in the brain. Standard psychiatric practice has been to discount the voices, or to ignore them, on the grounds that doing so reminds patients that they are not real and that their commands should not be followed. One might think of the standard approach as calling a spade a spade. But it is also true that when voices are imagined as agents, they are also imagined as having the ability to choose to stop talking. Members of the Hearing Voices network report that this is what they do. In 2009, at a gathering in the Dutch city of Maastricht, person after person diagnosed with schizophrenia stood up to tell the story of how they had learned to talk with their voices—and that their voices had then agreed to stop.

This lesson—that the world as imagined can change the world as it is—lies behind the intervention that helped Susan so much. In care-as-usual, people diagnosed with schizophrenia are regarded as severely disabled and thus, appropriate recipients of supported housing and other benefits. People are required to get their diagnosis to justify their placements, sometimes being asked to collect an actual piece of paper from one office and turn it in to another. Many people with schizophrenia cycle through long periods of homelessness. Few of them like it. You would think that they would line up to be housed. But in fact, they dislike the diagnosis even more than they do being out on the street, because the idea of being "crazy" seems even more horrifying to them than it does to those of us who have housing. For many months, I spent time with homeless women on the streets of Chicago who clearly met criteria for schizophrenia. They talked about going crazy as something the street did to people who were too weak to handle the life, and they thought of being crazy as having a broken brain that could never be fixed. And so they often refused to accept housing that required a psychiatric diagnosis, or they would take it for a while and then leave. They lived lives of restless nomadism, intermittently being hospitalized or jailed by the police when their behavior got out of hand, then released to supported housing, and finding their way back to the bleak streets in turn.

The new intervention simply gives people housing without asking them to admit to a diagnosis. Programs like the one that helped Susan are supported by federal funding set aside for the seriously mentally ill, but the benefit is not described that way to clients. Susan knows that she has subsidized housing, but she thinks she got it because she entered a program at a shelter to help her get off crack. Those who created the programs believe that the social setting in which she lives and imagines herself have as much to do with her treatment as any medication. In general, the data proves that they are right. People are more likely to accept housing when offered it in these programs than in care-as-usual settings, and after they are housed, their symptoms lessen—whether or not they are taking medications.

In part this backlash against the bio-bio-bio model reflects the sophisticated insight of a new emerging understanding of the body—*epigenetics*—in which genes themselves respond to an individual's social context. There is even an effort within psychiatry to abandon diagnosis altogether, and instead focus on dimensions of specific behaviors, like fear or working memory. Realistically, this project—the Research Domain Criteria—won't dismantle the diagnostic edifice. Too much of the structure of reimbursement and care depends upon the fiction of clear-cut, biologically distinct diseases. Still, the scientists are trying.

But the pushback is also a return to an older, wiser understanding of mind and body. In his *Second Discourse,* Jean-Jacques Rousseau describes human beings as made up out of each other through their interactions, their shared language, their intense responsiveness. "The social man, always outside of himself, knows only how to live in the opinions of others; and it is, so to speak, from their judgment alone that he draws the sentiment of his own existence." We are deeply social creatures. Our bodies constrain us, but our social interactions make us who we are. The new, more socially complex approach to human suffering simply takes that fact seriously again.

TANYA LUHRMANN is a psychological anthropologist best known for her studies of modern-day witches, charismatic Christians, and psychiatrists. She holds a Ph.D. from the University of Cambridge and is the Watkins University Professor in the Stanford Anthropology Department. This article was originally published in *Wilson Quarterly,* 2012.

III

Restraint

Stephanie Stewart-Bailey, *Utica Crib* (2012)
Exploratorium visitors imagine themselves as caregiver and patient at the *Restraint* installation.

Pamela Winfrey

RESTRAINT: LET ME COUNT THE WAYS

The third area of *The Changing Face of What is Normal* is an installation entitled *Restraint.* It began as an Exploratorium experiment: we were attempting to push on the idea of an interactive exhibit. In our institution, interactivity in a "traditional" sense often involves pushing buttons, sliding levers, turning dials, and then observing the results—lights go on, colors change, sound modulates. Recently, however, a group of exhibit developers and curators have been focusing on *humans* as phenomena, and in the new exhibits we're developing, we try to prompt visitors to closely observe other people and to reflect on their own thoughts, feelings, and social behavior. We're asking the public to think about how they fit into the greater world of humans, and then to step back and think about *how* they think, to question why they react to their social surroundings as they do.

In *Restraint,* we ask people to lie in a cage-like object called the Utica Crib. It's a replica of a real device used in 19th-century psychiatric institutions to prevent patients from harming themselves or others. People who found themselves in these kinds of facilities (many very much like Willard) were often there because their behavior strayed outside of what society at the time deemed *normal.* In this installation, we ask people to imagine what it would be like to be put in that cage involuntarily. People enclosed in the Crib could not turn over or bring their legs to their chest; they could only stare upward, exposed, not in control, forced into one position for hours, perhaps days. It did calm some patients. How would you react?

However, the installation also urges visitors to think about the concept of restraint in other ways. In addition to the Crib, the area displays a straitjacket and a video loop of pills spilling endlessly on a conveyor belt in a pharmaceutical plant. But restraints don't have to be physical or chemical; they can also be legal, social, or psychological. The most crucial element in this room is the visitor comment area where visitors contribute their own thoughts about the myriad ways they feel restrained in their everyday lives—by the assumptions of others, by societal and cultural rules, by their expectations of themselves.

Like many interactive exhibits, this installation is a prompt for continued experimentation and reflection in the world beyond the museum's walls. Restraints are common in any society, and many go unnoticed. Laws require that we carry certain kinds of identification. Borders and security zones regulate our movements. There are reasons for such restrictions, but one doesn't need to break a law to feel the restraining power of everyday social and cultural norms. Sit down in the middle of the floor at the mall, face the wrong way in an elevator, stand a bit too close to another person, act in an age-inappropriate manner, and people will tell you in word or deed what they think of your transgression. (Such is the ingrained power of social norms that you may even feel your pulse race and beads of sweat on your brow before anyone gives you a glance.) But when does the failure to meet a given societal or cultural expectation move from a minor breach to a reason for taking away someone's freedom? If we are seen as operating beyond certain unwritten rules, we might find ourselves in a lockdown facility for 48 hours of observation. What happens then?

VISITOR RESPONSES TO *RESTRAINT*

These comments were typewritten by visitors at an early presentation of *Restraint*. Visitors were asked to reflect on the many ways—physical, social, psychological—that they have felt restrained or limited in their lives.

‌GGFᵀ...:@?½⅓)('&_7#"EEEEE

ey there,
I feel restrained by the secular values of this
world. Why do I need to get married? Do I have to g

get kids? Why do I have to be skinny? Why can I

not eat my heart out. I feelrestrained.

J.A.Salazar

I want so badly to rit e my story to he lp
                         e

othe sheal from their abuse, except I am too

afraid to cause shame to the one who has

abused me for my whole life.

Restraint means differeny
(different) things to
different people. In my
eyes, it is about keeping
calm when you face a
frustrating task.
A task might be as simple
as figurin out how
to use a typewriter
It can be very
frustrating, but you
have to show
restraint and pull
through. You wont
be good at anything
if you don;t show
much restraint.

at times i feel restrained by life

well..the circumstanc4s of life

finances...lack of truth from others

lack of stimuli..lack of..the spark

that keeps one moving. sometimes i slow

down, and i know its not my true nature.

i need to get back on the horce. i need

to relight the spark. i need to get back t

to me.

I HATE BE NO TERIOTYPED AS AMISH. NO ONE REALLY KNOWS HOW WE
FEEL. THEY THINK THAT WE ARE JUST TORIST ATTRACKTIONS.
    I DONT KNOW WHERE I AM IN LIFE AND NO ONE KOWS HAT. NOT
EVEN MY CLOSEST FRIENDS. MOST PEOPLE THINK THAT IM PERFECT UNT
THEY GET TO KNOW ME, THEN THEY THINK THAT IM THE WORST PERS N
EVE... I AM NEITHER AND I HOPE PEOPLE WILL REALIZE THAT...IDK

LOVE VIOLET

PS... I WILL AND OTHERS WILL LEARN TO SEE OTHE S AS THEY REALLY

ARE EVENTUALLY... LIFE GOES ON... :)

I feel restrained by my ister she wont let
me gto bed at nigt and i am sleepy

                         n

RESTRAINT COMES IN MANY FORMS

Our behaviors, thoughts, and emotions are restrained in many ways, not all of them tangible. Laws and regulations constrain our actions, but so do addictions, unwritten social norms, and cultural boundaries.

Pete Pin, *Displaced: The Cambodian Diaspora* (2011)
Thon Khoun, 47, cooks in the kitchen of her Bronx apartment. Mrs. Khoun immigrated to the United States as a refugee in 1985. She is a single mother of four. Like many Cambodian refugees, she speaks no English and her children cannot speak Khmer. These limitations create linguistic boundaries that isolate her socially.

Photograph courtesy of Vicki and Chuck Rogers (2006)
Even in a place many perceive to be liberal and free-spirited, such as Santa Cruz, California, laws and regulations constrain our behaviors.

Courtesy of Bettmann/*Corbis, Man Feeling Hoodlums During Detroit Race Riot* (1943)
An African American man tries to escape from violent white attackers during a riot. In America's continuing struggle over civil rights, many people—some known, but many forever anonymous—have paid a terrible price for breaking prejudicial social rules about "normal" behavior.

Courtesy of Miguel Gandert/Corbis, *Gamblers at Slot Machine* (1997)
Addictions such as gambling can prevent people from living the lives they want to live

James Wakefield, *Jane & Debbie* (2005)
Jane and Debbie are post-operative male-to-female transsexuals living together, in a relationship.
According to the National Coalition of Anti-Violence Programs, transgender women made up 40% of the 30
reported hate murders in 2011, while representing only 10% of total hate crime survivors and victims. Many
transgender people feel they must keep their identities confidential to remain safe.

Bullit Marquez/AP/Courtesy of Corbis, *Markina Museum, Luzon Island, Philippines* (2012)
Some mental health professionals have proposed that compulsive buying could qualify as a distinct disorder,
along with other behavioral addictions such as internet addiction and compulsive gambling.

Exploratorium
Chris Cerrito
Hugh E. McDonald
Bill Meyer
Kerri Mullen
Tom Rockwell
Pete Scheidl
Stephanie Stewart-Bailey
Pamela Winfrey
Mary Elizabeth Yarbrough

Contributors
Susan Carlisle
Chris Carroll
Eugene Carroll
Andrea Craver
Jon Crispin
Sarah (Sally) Dawley
Jane Dox
Peg Ellsworth
Jim Goldberg
Tanya Luhrmann
Hugh E. McDonald
Karen L. Miller
Julie Prentice
Webb Rankin
Peggy Ross
Jader Tadefa
Paul (Jerry) Westervelt
Craig Williams
Pamela Winfrey
David Allyn Young
Sally Zinmann

Consultants
Mira A. Carberry
Susan Henderson
Allen Horwitz
Helena Kraemer
Karen L. Miller
Susan Miller

Book Design
Jon Sueda, Stripe SF

Production
Susan Miller

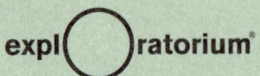

The Exploratorium is a global leader in informal learning, igniting curiosity and inspiring creativity in people of all ages. The museum creates original, interactive exhibits on display at more than 1,000 science centers, museums and public spaces around the world. Dedicated to education reform in and out of the classroom, the Exploratorium is a professional development center for educators and a creator of award-winning educational resources. For more information, visit exploratorium.edu.